D1260642

The Red Tails

WORLD WAR II'S
TUSKEGEE AIRMEN

By Steven L. Jones

Perfection Learning®

About the Author

Steve Jones lives in Ames, Iowa, with his wife, Diane. They are the parents of three sons: Danny, Mike, and Ben. Steve has a bachelor's degree in journalism from Iowa State University and a master's degree in communication from the University of Northern Iowa.

Steve is also the author of *Football's Fallen Hero: The Jack Trice Story.*

Acknowledgments

This book is dedicated to the Tuskegee Airmen. They overcame prejudice and discrimination to help defend the United States during World War II. These American heroes are an inspiration to all.

A special thanks goes to John Adelmann, other staff members, and the students at Central Alternative High School in Dubuque, Iowa. Their research and resulting book, *The Tuskegee Airmen—Victory at Home and Abroad,* was an invaluable resource for this book.

Image Credits: arttoday.com pp. 4, 5, 14, 15, 16, 23, 30, 31, 44, 46, 53, 58, 60; Corbis pp. 10, 11, cover; Digital Stock pp. 13, 20, 24, 25, 34, 36, 37, 39, 40, 41, 42, 43, 48, 52, 55, 56–57; Library of Congress pp. 6, 7, 8, 9, 17, 18, 19, 21, 35; National Air and Space Museum, Smithsonian Institution pp. 27, 28, 32, 45

Cover Design: Tobi Cunningham
Inside Design: Tobi Cunningham

TABLE *of* CONTENTS

TUSKEGEE, ALABAMA

In late 1939, Germany was waging war in Europe. Germany conquered Poland in September. Other nations would soon fall. Death and destruction were widespread. Millions of people were losing their freedom.

Japan was fighting on the other side of the world. The Japanese had invaded China. More people were dying. Millions more were losing their freedom.

This was the beginning of World War II.

Many people believed the United States would be drawn into the war. So the U.S. started training more troops. Ships and airplanes were built.

Military leaders needed a supply of young men to fly fighter planes, bombers, and other aircraft. So the U.S. Congress passed a law to establish pilot training programs across the country.

Factory workers building airplanes

Most of the pilot training schools were at colleges and universities. Some colleges were mostly for African Americans. So a number of blacks earned their pilot's licenses.

Joseph Gomer earned his pilot's license while attending a college in Iowa. In fact, he learned to fly before he could drive a car!

"I rode a bicycle out to the airport," Gomer said. His family did not own a car. "It was a small town, and you really didn't need a car," he explained.

Many young black men, like Gomer, became excellent pilots. But they could not fly in the military. The U.S. Army Air Corps did not accept African Americans.

The United States military was **segregated**. Blacks were kept separate from whites. They were not allowed to hold important combat positions.

Most of the time, blacks became cooks, truck drivers, and laborers. Those qualified for advanced jobs could not have them.

It seemed odd to many people that blacks could not fight for their country. Blacks had volunteered for U.S. military service for nearly 200 years.

They fought against the British in the Revolutionary War and the War of 1812. African Americans also served in the Union army during the Civil War. They served with the U.S. Cavalry in the late 1800s and fought in World War I.

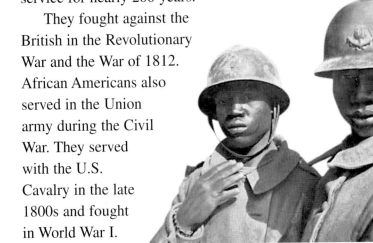

Many young men wanted to become Army Air Corps pilots. It was a glamorous job. And people looked up to them. Pilots proudly wore their wings on their uniforms.

But the military did not believe African Americans would make good pilots.

The Army Air Corps based its policies on a 1925 study of blacks in war. The report said blacks were lazy. And they lacked courage. It also stated blacks were not good military leaders. They should not be in combat.

Military leaders approved the misguided study. They considered blacks to be second-class citizens. But they were just reflecting what much of the rest of the country felt.

Prejudice against African Americans was strong, especially in the South. It was not unusual for blacks to be kept from entering cafes, theaters, and hotels.

Often there were separate rest rooms, dining rooms, and even drinking fountains for blacks. African Americans had to sit in the rear of buses. On trains, they sat in "Negroes Only" cars.

Discrimination was found in other regions of the country as well. Blacks had trouble getting good jobs. And they could not live in certain neighborhoods.

Despite this **racism**, blacks wanted to fly for their country. By 1940, several African American organizations pressured the government.

In addition, a black college student filed a lawsuit. He asked the courts to force the U.S. military to accept black pilot cadets.

Years later, a black pilot asked, "Can you imagine a citizen of the United States having to sue so he could fly and fight and die for his country?"

Soon, military policies changed. In early 1941, the Army Air Corps established an all-black flying outfit. It was named the 99th Pursuit **Squadron**. Cadets were going to learn to fly fighter planes like the P-40 Warhawk.

The military also decided to train its first black pilots in a little town deep in the South. Tuskegee (Tuss-KEY-gee), Alabama, was home to a small college for black students, Tuskegee Institute. The college had a strong aviation program. It would help train the pilots. Construction of an Army Air Corps base would soon begin six miles from town.

The Tuskegee pilots needed men to service their planes. So the Army Air Corps decided to train black mechanics and other ground crewmen at an airfield in Rantoul, Illinois.

The stage was finally set for black men to prove they could fly in the Army Air Corps.

Tuskegee Institute

FIRST LADY AT TUSKEGEE

In 1940, Eleanor Roosevelt visited Tuskegee Institute. She was the wife of President Franklin D. Roosevelt. Mrs. Roosevelt had been invited to see the flight program and help raise money.

She met Tuskegee's chief flight instructor, Charles Alfred "Chief" Anderson. She told Anderson, "Some say Negroes can't fly airplanes, but you seem to be flying around very well."

Then, against the wishes of her aides, she climbed into Anderson's plane. They flew over the campus. She enjoyed the ride. A photo of Mrs. Roosevelt and Anderson appeared in newspapers throughout the nation.

Anderson said that the plane ride and photo brought lots of positive attention to black aviation.

THE "EXPERIMENT"

Tuskegee was a small, rural town in eastern Alabama. It had about 4,000 residents. Tuskegee Institute was the town's most famous landmark. This historic college opened July 4, 1881. It was one of the early institutions that educated blacks in the South.

Tuskegee's first president was Booker T. Washington. He was a former slave. Washington served 34 years at Tuskegee until his death in 1915. He was one of the United States' most well-known black educators.

Some people were pleased that Tuskegee was chosen for the pilot program. Some thought it honored Washington.

Booker T. Washington

But others were unhappy. They questioned why the first all-black flying outfit was located in the South. The cadets would face racism and prejudice. Many black leaders believed the military wanted to see the black flying squadron fail.

Some military leaders viewed the entire plan as an "experiment." They doubted that blacks could become fighter pilots.

But hundreds of blacks still wanted an opportunity to try to earn their wings. Applications for Tuskegee came pouring in. Most of these men were highly qualified. Many had college degrees from top universities.

Some applicants scored so high on their military entrance tests that they were suspected of cheating. A few had to retake their exams.

The first pilot trainees arrived in Tuskegee in July 1941. Thirteen members formed the first group, called class 42C. These young men included a policeman, a U.S. Military Academy graduate, a musician, and former athletes.

They attended a dedication ceremony July 19. Army Air Corps General Walter Weaver spoke to the trainees.

"The eyes of your country and the eyes of your people are upon you. The success of the venture depends upon you," Weaver said.

The pilot trainees were excited and proud. But it was not until years later that these young men fully realized they were making history.

Army Air Corps training was divided into three parts: primary, basic, and advanced. The first class began training at Tuskegee Institute. Further training took place at the new air base near town.

Black air corps cadets spent a lot of time on the base. They were not welcome everywhere in the town of Tuskegee. Restaurants and the town movie theater had separate "colored" areas. Some cafes would sell food to blacks but not let them eat it in the dining rooms.

Whites stayed on one side of the town square, African Americans on the other. It was especially hard for blacks to find housing in town.

But the cadets had little time to think of anything other than their training. They all wanted their wings. They worked hard to prove the "experiment" would work.

chapter

FLIGHT TRAINING

It was quite a feat to become a U.S. fighter pilot. Most who tried—whites and blacks—failed. The fast, propeller-powered fighter planes carried only one person. Pilots had to fly, navigate, drop bombs, and fire the guns. Fighter pilots were very skilled.

Military pilot training was difficult and tiring. It was stressful. Cadets had to learn a lot in a short time. They were under a lot of pressure.

Many trainees were *washed out*. This meant cadets were dropped from the program. They had failed one or more parts of the training. If cadets failed a test or showed a bad attitude, they could be shipped out. And they had to be good flyers too.

Most of all, the cadets had to follow orders. Disobeying orders was probably the quickest way to be washed out. Instructors said there was only one way to do something. That was the army way!

The instructors were good, but they were tough. One pilot cadet recalled what a white flight instructor had told his unit. "Look at the man to your left and the one to your right. These two men will not complete the training."

The instructor was telling the trainees that two of every three cadets would probably wash out.

The first Tuskegee flight instructors were white. As tough as they were, most cadets thought they were fair. These instructors had volunteered for duty at Tuskegee. They wanted to be there.

The instructors had good students to work with. The Tuskegee pilot trainees were bright and well-educated. They were eager to learn. **Morale** was high.

The trainees supported one another. Their success would look good for blacks everywhere, especially blacks in aviation.

After a few weeks of training, only five trainees remained. Eight of the first thirteen members had been washed out. The five trainees were Lemuel Custis of Connecticut; Charles DeBow of Indiana; George Roberts of West Virginia; Mac Ross of Ohio; and Benjamin Davis, Jr., who had lived in several states.

PT-17

Their first planes were simple trainers, PT-17s. These were biplanes with two wings, one on top of the other. They looked like World War I planes. They were slow and easy to fly.

The instructor flew with the trainees at first. Even if the trainee had a pilot's license, the instructor went along. He taught the trainees to take off and land, control the plane in the air, and deal with emergencies.

After several hours of flight, the trainees were permitted to solo. This was the first time new pilots flew by themselves. The solo was a big event in a pilot's life.

Custis remembered his first solo as "the first step in a long journey." It was a proud moment for him.

Next the trainees moved to BT-13s. They were larger, single-wing aircraft. Soon the pilots flew AT-6s. These were even bigger trainers. They had larger engines and flew more like fighter planes.

BT-13

P-40 Warhawk

The five trainees soon moved up to their first fighters, the P-40 Warhawks. They were fast, nimble planes. They carried machine guns and could drop bombs.

The young pilots were in the middle of training when they heard shocking news. On a quiet Sunday morning, December 7, 1941, the Japanese attacked the Pearl Harbor Naval Base in Hawaii.

The surprise attack killed 2,400 Americans. Eighteen ships suffered heavy damage. Almost 200 airplanes were destroyed or badly damaged.

The next day, President Franklin D. Roosevelt addressed the nation on radio. The United States has declared war on Japan, he said. War was also declared on Germany and Italy.

The U.S. was fighting on the side of the Allies. By the end

Franklin D. Roosevelt

of the war, the Allies included Great Britain, France, the Soviet Union (now Russia), and many other nations.

The enemies were the Axis nations. They included Germany, Japan, and Italy. It would be a long, terrible war.

By early 1942, the new pilots were perfecting their flying abilities. They practiced new, difficult maneuvers. They worked on emergency landings and flew at night. They were becoming good pilots.

Fighter aircraft had several uses. They dropped bombs and protected U.S. bombers from enemy planes. They also **strafed** enemy targets. *Strafing* was low-level machine-gun attacks on ground targets.

Finally, the long training was over. All the cadets' hard work had paid off. On March 7, 1942, five young men marched onto the Tuskegee runway.

In a formal ceremony, silver wings were pinned on their uniforms. Lemuel Custis, Charles DeBow, George Roberts, Mac Ross, and Benjamin Davis, Jr., had successfully completed pilot training.

Four were promoted from cadet to second lieutenant in the U.S. Army Air Force (the new name for the Army Air Corps). The fifth man was Davis. He already was an army captain. He had graduated from the U.S. Military Academy in 1936.

UNITED STATES AIR FORCE

In 1947, the U.S Army Air Force became the U.S. Air Force. It was no longer a part of the army. The air force was now an independent branch of the armed forces.

The Army Air Force's five newest fighter pilots were black. They were probably the military's proudest pilots too. In the following weeks and months, other classes of black pilots graduated. Soon, the 99th Fighter Squadron (the name was changed during training) was at full strength.

In May 1942, the air force activated the 100th Fighter Squadron at Tuskegee. It was the second all-black fighter outfit. Mac Ross was named commander of the 100th.

Davis was given command of the 99th. He also was promoted to major, then lieutenant colonel. It was a high rank. He was deserving of the honor.

chapter

BENJAMIN O. DAVIS

It was no surprise that Benjamin O. Davis, Jr., was named to lead the Army Air Force's 99th Fighter Squadron. He was an intelligent and hardworking officer. He was an outstanding leader.

Benjamin Davis was born in 1912 in Washington, D.C. His father was Benjamin O. Davis, Sr. The older Davis was an army officer. He would became the nation's first African American general.

The younger Davis's mother died when he was four years old. His father remarried and the family settled in Tuskegee, Alabama. The older Davis taught military science at Tuskegee Institute. The family later moved to Cleveland, Ohio.

Benjamin O. Davis, Jr.

As a teenager, Davis spent a summer with relatives in Washington, D.C. While at the nation's capital, he watched an air show. He really enjoyed watching planes do acrobatic spins and dives. Before long, Davis knew he wanted to fly.

Davis graduated from Central High School in Cleveland. He was an excellent student. He was elected president of the school's student council.

He started college in the Cleveland area. However, Davis's father wanted him to attend the U.S. Military Academy in West Point, New York. This is a college where future army officers are educated.

But Davis was unsure about West Point. He had heard that African Americans were not treated well at the academy. None had graduated from West Point since Charles Young in 1889. Davis also did not like the segregated army.

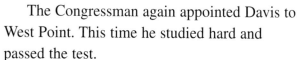

However, Davis decided to give West Point a try. He moved to Illinois so a black Chicago Congressman could nominate him to the academy.

Davis still had to take a tough entrance test to get in to West Point. He already had more than a year of college. He believed he would have little trouble passing the test.

He was wrong. Davis failed the test. But it was his failure that motivated him to do better.

The Congressman again appointed Davis to West Point. This time he studied hard and passed the test.

Charles Young

Davis entered the academy in 1932. But his four years there were difficult. He was discriminated against by the all-white corps of cadets. Many did not want blacks at the academy.

Davis endured *silencing*. This meant no other cadet talked to him unless necessary. Davis also had no roommate his entire four years. It was a lonely time for him. He said later that he was an "invisible man" at West Point.

Instead of complaining, Davis worked harder. He could not be forced to quit the academy. Years later, Davis wrote, "I was silenced solely because cadets did not want black cadets at West Point. Their only purpose was to freeze me out."

U.S. Military Academy in West Point, New York

But Davis said the other cadets did not know how stubborn he was. He was going to put up with their treatment. He was going to stay and graduate.

The summer before his senior year, Davis spent time at an Army Air Corps base. He rode in some airplanes. He truly enjoyed flying.

That fall, Davis applied for the Army Air Corps. He decided he would rather fly than be in the infantry.

Davis easily passed the physical test required of pilots. However, he soon heard bad news—he was rejected. The Army Air Corps had no plans for black pilots.

Davis graduated in 1936. He did very well in school—his grades ranked him 35th in his class of 236 cadets. He also became an army second lieutenant. Following graduation, Davis married and was sent to Georgia in the segregated South. He was in the army, but he never lost his desire to fly.

Over the next five years, Davis rose to the rank of captain. Then he was transferred to Tuskegee Institute. He commanded an officer training program at the college. Later, he was shipped to a Kansas army post.

Davis and his wife had just settled in Kansas when good news arrived. Captain Davis had been assigned to a new all-black flying unit at Tuskegee, Alabama. His dream of flying had been answered.

chapter 5

WAITING

The 99th Fighter Squadron continued training at Tuskegee. The fourth class of pilots graduated in July 1942.

Lieutenant Colonel Benjamin Davis spoke at the ceremony. He said the Tuskegee training prepared the men well. Now they must do their job "in the air against the enemy," he added.

The mechanics and other ground crew stationed in Rantoul, Illinois, joined the pilots. For every pilot, there were at least ten men and women on the ground in support roles.

The ground crew included mechanics, weather forecasters, medical staff, cooks, and others. The ground crew was vital to the success of the pilots.

The 99th was now at full strength. The men were combat ready. However, the military did not have a plan for them. The squadron remained in Tuskegee.

Davis worked the pilots hard to perfect their combat skills. They had to perform well in everything they did. If not, future opportunities for black aviators would be limited.

Flying P-40s, the 99th practiced bomb runs, took target practice, and worked on their navigation skills. They earned commendations for their flying.

But morale was low at Tuskegee. The men were anxious to fight. But all they did was train. White pilots with the same training were sent overseas to war.

Making conditions worse was a new base commander. He strictly enforced military segregation. Signs indicating "white" and "colored" appeared on base rest rooms and elsewhere. In addition, the base was overcrowded.

At the beginning of 1943, the 99th and 100th fighter squadrons were still in Tuskegee. But a new base commander took over. Colonel Noel Parrish made several favorable changes. He had the "white" and "colored" signs removed.

Parrish helped get black singers and actors to entertain at Tuskegee. World heavyweight boxing champion Joe Louis, an African American, also visited. Racial tensions eased under Parrish. He was a strong supporter of African Americans in military aviation.

Morale improved, but the 99th remained in Tuskegee. African American leaders tried to persuade the War Department to send the 99th into combat.

Some feared that the military was permitting its "Tuskegee experiment" to fail. Before long the 99th noticed some differences. Their

Singer Lena Horne and Col. Noel Parrish with Tuskegee Airmen

training was stepped up. Combat flying practice increased.

Finally, word came on April 1, 1943. The 99th was shipping out. It had been more than a year since the first class of pilots graduated from flight training. Saying good-bye to well-wishers, the men boarded a train in Tuskegee. They traveled to Brooklyn, New York.

On April 15, they boarded a troop ship, the U.S.S. *Mariposa*. More than 3,000 soldiers were on board.

Thirteen days later, the 99th Fighter Squadron landed in Casablanca, Morocco. They were in North Africa. Soon they would test their skills in war.

chapter

6

COMBAT!

North Africa is a vast, sandy desert. It was the scene of many terrible battles early in the war. When the 99th Fighter Squadron arrived, the fighting there was nearly over. The Allies had pushed almost all the Germans out of North Africa.

The 99th set up a temporary training camp in the hot desert. All the camp had was a dirt runway. The men pitched tents and went to work.

Then good news arrived. The pilots were getting their airplanes. And they were new P-40 Warhawks! They were much nicer than the old P-40s they used in training. These planes had advanced engines and could fly faster.

The 99th spent May 1943 training with the 27th Fighter Group from a nearby base. (Several squadrons make up one fighter group.) The 27th welcomed the black airmen. The two fighter outfits engaged in practice dogfights. *Dogfights* were aerial combats among aircraft.

The training with the 27th was important. Most **rookie** fighter squadrons had combat-experienced pilots assigned to teach them. But because the military was segregated, no black pilots had yet been in combat.

After a month of training, the 99th was assigned to the 33rd Fighter Group. They relocated at a new camp, a former German airfield in Tunisia.

On June 2, 1943, the squadron flew its first combat mission. The pilots in their new P-40s strafed targets on the Italian island of Pantelleria. Little happened on the first few missions. The black pilots saw no enemy aircraft. They wondered when they would encounter the Germans.

Lieutenant Colonel Benjamin Davis knew his pilots were ready. He believed no flying unit would go into battle as well trained as the 99th. These pilots had more flying time prior to combat than most.

However, none of the men had combat experience, including Davis. The combat came soon enough.

Me-109s

A week after their first mission, the pilots were escorting bombers back to base. All of a sudden, German Messerschmitt-109s came soaring out of the sun. The Me-109s (pronounced "M-E") were good airplanes. They were faster than the P-40s.

Some of the black pilots chased the enemy planes. They exchanged gunfire. Lieutenants Charles Dryden and Spann Watson hit a pair of Me-109s.

Lieutenant Willie Ashley attacked another plane. The Me-109 started losing altitude. Ashley followed it as it fell toward earth. But he lost sight of the plane.

Ashley could not confirm that the plane had been destroyed. U.S. pilots only were credited with shooting down an enemy plane when they knew for sure it had crashed.

B IS FOR BOMBER

United States military planes are classified by a letter and number. The letter is the type of aircraft and the number is the model. For example, the *B* in B-24 is for bomber. The *P* in P-40 is for pursuit aircraft. Other letters include *C* for cargo, *T* for trainer, and *A* for attack plane. Modern airplanes also include *F* for fighter and *K* for tanker.

In June, the 99th helped the Allies capture Pantelleria and two smaller islands. The next step was to capture Sicily, a large island near Italy.

During a bomber escort mission in July, Lieutenant Charles Hall saw enemy fighters. They were German Focke-Wulf-190s. They were coming after the bombers.

Hall steered his plane into position and fired his machine guns. He hit an FW-190 in the side. Hall followed the damaged plane as it fell from the sky. He saw it hit the ground.

Hall had a confirmed victory. He became the first African American pilot to shoot down an enemy plane.

When he returned to base, Hall did a "victory roll" in his P-40. It signaled the ground crew that he had downed a German plane. The men were excited.

But their joy quickly ended. They soon learned that two of their own pilots were killed that day. Lieutenants Sherman White and James McCullin died in a midair collision.

In July 1943, the black pilots took part in the invasion of Sicily. They escorted Allied ships that carried troops to the island. In late July, the 33rd Fighter Group, including the Tuskegee Airmen, left North Africa. They set up a new base in Licata on the coast of Sicily.

Throughout July and August, the 99th flew many missions. They escorted bombers and strafed enemy positions. But the squadron recorded no more victories.

Eventually, the Allies had complete control of Sicily. Then in September, they landed in Italy at Salerno. New air bases were established. White fighter squadrons were sent to the area. But most of the 99th remained in Sicily.

The Germans soon launched a major offensive. A big battle took place, and the Allies stopped the Germans.

But the 99th missed the battle. The black pilots wondered why they had been left behind. They soon learned they had a battle to fight in the United States as well as in Europe.

chapter 7

BATTLE AT HOME

In early September 1943, Lieutenant Colonel Benjamin Davis received some surprising orders.

Davis was to return to the United States and take command of the all-black 332nd Fighter Group. Captain George "Spanky" Roberts was to remain in Europe and command the 99th.

The 332nd had trained at Tuskegee. Then the group went to Selfridge Field near Detroit, Michigan. The 332nd was made up of three fighter squadrons— the 100th, 301st, and 302nd.

When Davis returned to the U.S., he thought his job would be to prepare the 332nd for war. He quickly learned he had a more pressing problem.

Capt. George S. Roberts and Lt. Colonel Benjamin O. Davis, Jr.

Colonel William Momyer commanded the 33rd Fighter Group, which included the 99th. Momyer wrote a negative report about the 99th. He said the outfit was not as good as his other squadrons.

The 99th was not aggressive and did not work as a team, Momyer wrote. He also reported that black flyers did not have the **stamina** to be fighter pilots. Surprisingly, other air force officials approved the report.

One general added, "The Negro type has not the proper reflexes to make a first-class pilot."

The final report recommended that the 99th be removed from combat. And black flying squadrons should be assigned to U.S. coastal patrol.

The black pilots were not happy. They were trained for combat. They wanted to fight for their country.

Davis was really mad. He wondered why he was not told about the charges. He believed the Army Air Force report was based on racism.

On October 16, 1943, Davis met with a high-ranking government committee. He had to defend the 99th. But he also was defending all African Americans in the military.

Davis told the committee the 99th made mistakes at first. He said the pilots had no combat experience. But he said the

Members of the 332nd Fighter Group

mistakes were corrected. The pilots had learned to fly and fight as a team. They were aggressive, he said.

Davis explained why the pilots' stamina was low. Other fighter squadrons had replacement pilots. The 99th had none. The pilots flew as many as six missions a day. They had a right to be tired.

Colonel Davis said the 99th was a top fighter squadron. The men of the 99th wanted a fair chance to show what they could do in battle. Davis's testimony was convincing.

Finally, the Army Air Force decided the 99th should remain in combat. It also agreed to send the 332nd Fighter Group to Europe when it was ready. In addition, plans moved ahead for an all-black bomber group.

The committee also decided to study the effectiveness of black pilots. The study took about one year to complete. But the results were favorable. It said the 99th performed as well as the white P-40 units.

The black pilots' battle in the United States was won. But they still had a war to fight in Europe.

VICTORY ROLLS

World War II was in full force in late 1943 and early 1944. Fighting was raging on the Pacific Ocean and in Asia and Europe.

Americans at home were contributing to the war effort. As men went off to fight, women took jobs in factories. They made uniforms, airplanes, and everything else needed to win a war.

The 99th Fighter Squadron moved again in October 1943. The squadron was ordered to the Foggia area in eastern Italy. They joined the 79th Fighter Group.

The all-white 79th was commanded by Colonel Earl Bates. He welcomed the black airmen and recognized their talent and dedication.

Black and white pilots flew **integrated** missions. This was against Army Air Force policy. But it helped the Tuskegee Airmen.

The two squadrons dive-bombed and strafed several targets together. The black pilots learned a lot from the 79th pilots.

The Tuskegee Airmen were becoming confident pilots. But as good as they were, they still

LIVING IN TENTS

American air bases in Italy were not fancy. As Allied troops advanced into new territory, airfields were quickly set up.

Pilots and crews often lived in big tents. The tents could blow over in high winds.

Dirt was everywhere. And when rain came, the dirt turned to mud.

were not shooting down many enemy aircraft. Other squadrons were getting credit for victories. These were the top squadrons in the eyes of the Army Air Force.

In January 1944, the 99th and 79th squadrons moved again. They were sent to Capodichino Airfield on the western side of Italy.

On the morning of January 27, members of the 99th were patrolling the skies near Anzio. The Allies had just landed in Italy. Below them were ships along the Mediterranean coastline and thousands of troops on shore. The 99th was protecting the coastal area from enemy aircraft.

Captain Clarence Jamison led a group of 12 P-40s that day. Jamison scanned the skies above him. He noticed a German FW-190 diving toward Allied ships. Other 190s were following. The black flyers were outnumbered by the faster German fighters.

But Jamison's group went after the 190s. All their training in Tuskegee and Europe had prepared them well. They were ready for whatever the *Luftwaffe*, the German air force, could throw at them. The air battle had begun.

Lieutenant Robert Diez came in behind a German plane. Firing his machine guns, he shot down the 190. Lieutenants Clarence Allen and Howard Baugh both fired on another plane and shot it down.

Leon Roberts, also a lieutenant, followed another fighter at low altitude. He pulled his trigger, sending the plane into the ground. Lieutenant Henry Perry fired on another 190 and also recorded a victory.

Lieutenant Willie Ashley chased a 190 for miles. They were almost to Rome before Ashley's machine-gun bursts finally blew up the enemy plane. In just a few minutes, the black pilots shot down five German fighters and damaged others.

When the P-40s returned to base, the ground crew was surprised. They watched as five planes did victory rolls! The pilots and their crews cheered and celebrated.

Capt. Charles B. Hall

The victories did not end. In the afternoon, another beach patrol shot down three more enemy aircraft. Eight victories in one day!

The day ended on a sad note. The men learned one of their pilots had been killed in the battle.

The next morning, the success continued. Captain Charles Hall shot down two more German fighters. He now had three confirmed kills. Lieutenant Diez and Lieutenant Lewis Smith also shot down 190s. This meant more victory rolls.

By the end of the second day, the 99th had downed 12 enemy aircraft. They also were credited with some *probables*. These were planes that probably crashed after being damaged.

The men of the 99th were happy. They had been given a chance to fight. And they showed what they could do.

An Army Air Force general flew to the base and congratulated the men. He told them to keep shooting because they were doing such a good job. A national magazine ran an article about the 99th's success.

"Any outfit would have been proud of the 99th's record," the article reported. "Its victories stamped the final seal of excellence" on the squadron.

MORE BLACK SQUADRONS

The 332nd Fighter Group was still training at Selfridge Field in Michigan under Lieutenant Colonel Benjamin Davis. All the men trained hard and learned a lot. Davis's combat experience helped the pilots become better flyers.

Davis and the 332nd left Michigan in late 1943. They boarded a troop ship and sailed to Italy. The men were on the ship about four weeks. It made several stops along the way dropping off troops and supplies.

The fighter group set up at bases on the western side of Italy. But Davis was not happy. The 332nd was far removed from combat.

The pilots participated in some strafing missions. But they mostly flew unimportant missions. The pilots wanted to fight. That's why they joined the Army Air Force.

The black pilots also were unhappy with their fighter planes. They flew outdated P-39 Airacobras.

P-39 Airacobra

Mount Vesuvius

Like the P-40, the P-39 was slower than German fighters. It also had a small cockpit. Tall pilots were cramped inside. However, the P-39 did have more powerful guns than the P-40.

For about three months, the 332nd rarely saw German planes. And when they did, their P-39s were too slow to chase them.

About the only highlight at this time was seeing Mount Vesuvius. This volcano erupted in March 1944. At night, the pilots watched red-hot lava flow down the sides of the mountain. The volcano sent so much ash into the air that many missions were grounded.

"The ash sounded like rain when it came down on our tents," said Lieutenant Joseph Gomer. "It piled up like snow."

When the 332nd returned to the air, the pilots continued flying routine missions. They rarely saw enemy aircraft. Davis wanted his group to fly combat missions. Finally, the word came. The 332nd was getting its chance.

P-47 Thunderbolt

Davis was ordered to see the 15th Air Force's commanding officer. The commander wanted the 332nd to take on a new job—an important job.

United States bombers were flying deep into German territory. The B-17s and B-24s were dropping thousands of bombs on enemy targets.

The targets were often factories that made tanks and airplanes. Other targets included railroad yards and refineries that made the fuel for tanks and planes.

U.S. bombers attacked during the day. British bombers flew at night. The goal was to slow Germany's ability to fight.

But U.S. daylight bombing missions were costly. Many of the big long-range bombers were destroyed. Thousands of men lost their lives.

The four-engine B-17 and B-24 bombers were big and slow. Even though they had machine guns for protection, they were easy targets for enemy aircraft.

Another danger was *flak*, whirling pieces of metal. Huge cannons on the ground fired at the bombers. The exploding cannon shells sprayed flak throughout the sky.

U.S. fighter escorts could not protect bombers from flak. But they could keep German planes from feasting on the bombers.

The commanding officer asked Davis to lead his men on long-range escort missions. The general needed more fighter escorts. It was a dangerous assignment.

"Needless to say, I leaped at the opportunity," Davis recalled later. He knew escort missions were important for the Allies. And, finally, his men could show what they could do.

The group's P-39s were not good enough for long missions. So the commander agreed to equip the 332nd with P-47 fighters.

The P-47 Thunderbolt was nicknamed the "jug." It was much bigger and sturdier than the P-39 or P-40. It also could fly faster, farther, and higher. It was a match for the German fighters.

The 332nd also was sent to a new base at Ramitelli, on Italy's east side. There they joined other fighter groups of the 15th Air Force.

About this same time, Davis received another promotion. He was now Colonel Benjamin Davis.

The 332nd was pleased to get its P-47s. When the planes arrived, the men did not like the designs on the tails. The ground crew got out their paint and painted each tail bright red. From that time on, the black pilots were known as the *Red Tails*.

As the 332nd was adjusting to new aircraft, the war took a major turn. Before dawn on June 6, 1944, thousands of Allied troops landed on a French beach. It was D-Day! The Allies were landing in Europe. They could march toward Germany to end the war.

The Allies now were heading toward Germany from three directions. The Americans and British were fighting in France from the west and Italy from the south. The Soviet Union was pushing toward Germany from the east.

However, the war in Europe was far from over.

chapter

THE RED TAILS

Outfitted in P-47s, the 332nd began flying long-range bomber escort missions. On June 9, 1944, the 332nd was flying with B-17s and B-24s.

B-17

The big planes were going to bomb factories in Munich, Germany. After the Red Tails met the bombers, they flew together toward the target.

Soon, German Me-109s zeroed in on the bombers. Colonel Benjamin Davis ordered his men to attack. A big air battle took place thousands of feet above ground.

When the dogfight ended, five German planes had been shot down. Only one Red Tail had been lost. Most importantly, not one bomber was lost to German fighters.

The bombers completed their bomb run and started returning to Italy. Again they were attacked by German planes. And again, the 332nd protected the big bombers.

The mission was a success. The bomber commander praised the 332nd for outstanding flying. Colonel Davis was later presented a Distinguished Flying Cross for leading the fighters that day.

The 332nd flew more escort missions in June. Each time, the Red Tails did their job—no U.S. bombers were shot down by German fighters.

On June 25, the group earned a big prize. Several pilots were on a low-altitude strafing mission over Yugoslavia. On the way back to their base, they spotted a German destroyer in the Adriatic Sea. A *destroyer* is a large warship with many guns.

The Red Tails had no bombs, but they attacked the ship with machine guns. The ship's crew fired back.

Captain Wendell Pruitt dove toward the ship and pulled his trigger. His gunfire hit the destroyer, causing some damage. Then Lieutenant Gwynne Pierson came soaring in. He also blasted away at the ship.

All of a sudden the ship exploded and quickly sank. Pierson

NAME THAT PLANE

Fighter pilots named their airplanes, often after their mothers, girlfriends, or wives. Some names came from popular songs. Others carried the pilots' nicknames.

A few of the names used by the Tuskegee Airmen included "Skipper's Darlin'," "Stinky," "My Buddy," and "Kitten." Group commander Benjamin O. Davis flew a P-51 named "Bennie."

The names were painted on the sides of the planes.

must have hit the ship's weapons or fuel supplies.

Pruitt and Pierson returned to base and told their story. Some commanders did not believe them. How could two small planes with only machine guns sink a large ship? But the P-47s had wing cameras. The attack was recorded on film. It really had happened!

By the end of June, two changes took place. The 99th Fighter Squadron—the first outfit from Tuskegee—joined the 332nd. Then the black pilots heard they were getting new planes, the P-51 Mustang.

However, the 99th did not like joining the 332nd. The pilots

P-51 Mustang

believed putting all the black squadrons together was a form of segregation.

There was another problem. The 99th pilots were exhausted. They had been in combat for a long time.

Most white pilots returned to the United States after flying about 50 missions. However, there were few black replacement pilots. The Tuskegee Airmen generally flew more missions than white pilots. Some would have more than 100 missions by the war's end.

The flight surgeon grounded many of the 99th pilots. They needed a few days of rest.

chapter 11

HONORS

During the summer of 1944, the 332nd grew into one large fighter group. The pilots also adapted to the much faster P-51.

The P-51 Mustang was the favorite fighter of most U.S. pilots. The sleek plane was smaller than the P-47. It was not as durable. But it was better in most other categories.

The Mustang could fly about 450 miles per hour. It could outrun other propeller planes.

P-51 Mustang

P-51 Mustang

The P-51 could do fast turns and rolls to chase or evade enemy aircraft.

"It was the plane to fly," said Lieutenant Joseph Gomer. "It was a great aircraft."

The tails of the new P-51s also were painted bright red. The entire group of black pilots now had a special identity.

Each fighter group had its own special markings on its planes. For example, some had checkerboards on their tails. Others had stripes or a solid color.

With P-51s, the 332nd provided maximum protection for the bombers. The Red Tails flew all over southern and eastern Europe escorting the big four-engine planes.

The B-17s and B-24s were attacking well-defended targets. They were seeing a lot of enemy fighters and heavy flak. But the 332nd stayed right with the bombers.

In a mid-July mission, several Red Tails escorted bombers to German-held territory in France. A large group of enemy planes headed toward the bombers. Sighting the P-51s, the German pilots turned their planes to escape.

We Will Get You Home

A damaged bomber limping back to base was a "sitting duck" for German pilots. Crews were thankful for U.S. fighters who came to the rescue.

One time, a B-17 was hit by flak after dropping its bombs. The plane fell behind the other planes in its group.

Soon, two red-tailed P-51s came along. The B-17 crew heard one of the Red Tail pilots say over the radio, "Come on, big brother, we will get you home."

The P-51s stayed with the disabled plane until reaching friendly territory. "Call on us any time," the black pilot said as he flew off.

On another mission, a B-24 lost two of its four engines. The plane lost altitude. The crew tossed out the guns and ammunition to lighten the load. They had no protection.

The pilot called for help. Twelve minutes later several Red Tails in their P-51s came to the rescue.

"You the boys in trouble?" asked the black pilot. The Red Tails guided the plane to safety.

Another time, black pilots helped a B-24 hit by flak. The Red Tails flew ahead and located an airfield. The bomber crash-landed, but the crew survived.

"I do owe my life and the life of the crew to the black Red Tail flyers, and I am eternally grateful," said a gunner on the B-24.

The Red Tails went after the fleeing aircraft. Captain Joseph Elsberry destroyed one enemy plane. Then Elsberry shot down two more German planes. He recorded three air victories in one battle!

As summer turned to fall, bombers continued their massive attacks. Factories, submarine bases, airfields, oil refineries, and other targets were hit. The Red Tails were on many of these missions.

The black pilots also strafed ground targets. In late summer, they attacked several hundred parked German airplanes. The pilots had an easy time tearing up the *Luftwaffe* fighters and bombers. None of the German planes took off to defend their airfield.

The 332nd earned a reputation for bravery and outstanding flying. Bomber crews in the 15th Air Force were becoming aware of the Red Tails. They called them the "Red Tail Angels" because of their good aerial protection.

On September 10, the Army Air Force recognized the 332nd. Four generals attended the award ceremony. One of them was General Benjamin O. Davis, Sr.—Colonel Davis's father. The elder Davis proudly pinned the Distinguished Flying Cross on his son.

General Benjamin Davis, Sr. and Col. Benjamin Davis, Jr.

Three other pilots, including Captain Elsberry, also received the DFC. It was a proud day for the African American fighter group.

The 332nd pilots continued destroying enemy planes in the air and on the ground. But as well as they were performing, they still had losses. Several Red Tails were shot down by German planes or ground fire. Some pilots were able to parachute out. Others were not so lucky. They died in combat.

When pilots parachuted, or "bailed out," over German territory, they often were captured. They were sent to German P.O.W. (prisoner of war) camps. One Red Tail P.O.W. remembered being questioned by German officers. He was surprised how much they knew about the black pilots.

Pilots who evaded capture had to find their way back to their bases. Lieutenant Robert Martin's P-51 was hit by antiaircraft fire in March 1945. He had been on a strafing mission over an airfield in Yugoslavia.

With his plane on fire, Martin bailed out. He spent five

weeks in Yugoslavia.

"Four of those weeks were spent at a British-operated rescue mission for downed Allied airmen," Martin recalled years later. He said it was a good place to get clean clothes, some food, and rest.

Martin eventually got a ride to the Adriatic Sea coast. From there he was flown back to Italy.

PROTEST AT FREEMAN FIELD

The 477th Bombardment Group became the first all-black bomber outfit. The group was formed in early 1944. It flew the two-engine B-25, which was smaller than the B-17 and B-24.

The 477th pilots learned to fly these medium-range bombers at Tuskegee. Then they trained with their crew members at Selfridge Field, Michigan.

B-25

Because of military segregation, shortages of pilots and gunners made training difficult. It was like a football team practicing without a quarterback or center.

A more pressing problem, however, affected the men— racism. The commander of the 477th was white. He was a strict follower of the military's policy of racial segregation.

He made decisions that upset the black officers. For example, African Americans were not allowed in the Selfridge Field officers' club.

Officers' clubs were popular recreation sites. They gave officers a place to relax. The airmen could get something to eat or drink, and perhaps play billiards or cards.

Since 1940, the army had allowed any officer assigned to a base to use the officers' club there. However, the commander ignored the army regulation.

When racial problems worsened, the 477th moved to Godman Field, Kentucky. Here, black officers had a tiny officers' club. White officers used a nicer club at a nearby base. But Godman was not large enough for the bombers. A few months later, the outfit went to Freeman Field, Indiana.

The 477th commander said there would be two officers' clubs. Club number 1 was for officer trainees. Club number 2 was for supervisory and instructor officers. All the black officers were assigned to club 1 because most of them were trainees. White officers were assigned to club 2, which was nicer.

Black officers were unhappy. They again were being treated as second-class citizens. In March 1945 several of them tried entering club 2. The commander later warned them to stay out. Then the black airmen came up with a plan.

They decided to use nonviolent protest to bring attention to the problem. The African American officers decided to enter the club. If they were arrested, they would not argue. They would go quietly.

So, on April 5, 1945, several small groups of officers tried using club 2. These men were arrested. Over the next couple of nights, many more black officers were arrested.

Within a few days, all but three were released. The three were held longer because they entered the club after one of them bumped a superior officer. This was considered "using force."

The commander declared new orders about the clubs. Each officer—white and black—was to read the orders and sign them. Everyone did except for 101 black officers. They were arrested and kept under guard at another base.

Word of the arrests spread among black leaders and organizations. They demanded an army investigation. Within a few days, the officers were released. As punishment, they received letters of reprimand. These letters indicated the army was unhappy with the officers' behavior. Years later, the air force removed the letters from their official files.

The three men who used force to enter the club remained under arrest. They were later tried in a military court for disobeying an order. They were found not guilty. But one black officer was fined $150 for using force on a superior officer.

As a result of the protest, the commander of the 477th was relieved of his duties. The army said he had not handled the situation well.

The men who participated in the Freeman Field protest took a chance. They disobeyed orders, a serious offense in wartime. But they believed in what they were doing. All Army Air Force officers deserved fair and equal treatment, they said.

In the end, their protest led to better conditions for all black officers.

chapter

ON TO BERLIN

In early 1945, Allied troops were marching closer to Germany. The Allies were winning the war. But the fighting was far from over. Soldiers and others were still dying. Several Red Tail pilots were killed in action during this time.

In the Pacific war, American troops were inching toward Japan. They were taking island after island from the Japanese in bloody battles.

Back in Italy, bad weather canceled a number of January bombing missions. By February, the B-17s and B-24s were pelting oil refineries and other targets. They also had a new target—jet aircraft factories.

Germany was building two types of jet fighters—Me-163s and Me-262s. Me-163s were fast. But they burned a lot of fuel and had little range.

The Me-262s were better jet fighters. They could fly more than 500 miles per hour. So they were much faster than even the P-51s. Me-262s could appear out of nowhere because of their speed and then zoom away.

The Red Tails first saw jets in December 1944. Most of the pilots had never before seen a plane fly without a propeller.

There was no dogfight that day. But the pilots figured they would face the jets sometime. The speedy aircraft would challenge the Red Tails.

By March 1945, the black pilots had collected several more victories. They earned praise for providing excellent protection for the bombers. The 332nd pilots were awarded many medals.

You'll Have the Best

Roger Jones was a B-24 nose gunner. He was in a preflight briefing with other bomber crews. An officer announced the day's mission—the railroad yards at Vienna, Austria.

B-24

Vienna was a well-defended target. It would be a tough mission, Jones thought.

The officer added, "You'll have the best protection in the 15th Air Force—the colored pilots."

Jones heard some grumbling from a couple of crews. For some reason, they did not want fighter protection from black pilots.

The officer raised his voice to quiet the men. "They are the best by record in the 15th Air Force bar none. That's why we're sending them with you."

Jones flew about half his missions with the Red Tails.

B-17s

Throughout the 15th Air Force, the reputation of the Red Tails was growing. They were known as skilled, disciplined pilots who knew how to do their job.

In late March, the Red Tails learned they would be part of a special bombing mission. It was a long and dangerous mission to Berlin, the German capital. The target was a tank factory.

The Berlin mission was a 1,600-mile round-trip from Italy. The bombers would spend about 10 hours in the air. It would end up being one of the 15th Air Force's longest missions.

The plan called for the 332nd to join the bombers near Berlin. The Red Tails' job was to escort the bombers to a designated location. Then they would turn over the protection to other fighters.

The mission started as planned. The planes crossed the snowcapped Alps mountains and continued north. As they neared Berlin, their orders were changed. The black pilots were now to stay with the bombers and go to the target.

After the bombers hit the tank factory, they headed back to Italy. The Red Tails were still with them. Before long, enemy fighters came soaring toward the American planes. They were Me-262s—the jets.

Despite being low on fuel and ammunition, the Red Tails fought the jets. The 262s were indeed fast. But they were not highly maneuverable. Also, U.S. pilots quickly learned the jet pilots did not have nearly the combat flying experience they had.

The big battle continued. Waves of 262s tried to attack the bombers. But the Red Tails were successful. They destroyed three jets and damaged others. However, three Tuskegee Airmen were killed in the battle.

But the Red Tails did it again. They did not lose a single bomber under their protection. Their record was still perfect.

The 332nd Fighter Group was awarded the Distinguished Unit Citation for its heroic mission. Perhaps more important, the Red Tails continued to earn the respect of more and more bomber crews.

A week after the Berlin mission, the black pilots again were in a large aerial battle. The Red Tails fought jets and propeller-powered fighters. It turned out to be the black pilots' biggest day. They recorded 13 victories!

In late April, the black pilots fought their last major air battle. They destroyed four German aircraft over the Mediterranean Sea. The Red Tails flew their final combat mission a few days later, on April 30.

A week later, May 7, 1945, Germany surrendered. The horrible war in Europe was over.

chapter 14

MILITARY INTEGRATION

Within the next few weeks and months, the 332nd Fighter Group returned to the U.S. Although the fighting in Europe ended, the war with Japan continued.

Colonel Benjamin Davis was given command of the troubled all-black 477th Composite Group. It formerly was called the 477th Bombardment Group. This outfit now had fighter planes in addition to B-25 bombers.

The 477th started training to fight Japan in the Pacific. (The 477th never went to Europe and had no combat record.)

Then startling events occurred. The Allies asked Japan to surrender. But Japan refused.

B-29

So in the early morning of August 6, 1945, a B-29 bomber headed toward Japan. When the plane was over the city of Hiroshima, out dropped a single bomb. But this was no ordinary explosive. It was an atomic bomb.

The bomb destroyed more than half of Hiroshima. Thousands of people died.

Japan again refused to surrender. Three days later, another B-29 dropped a second atomic bomb on Nagasaki. Again, most of that city was flattened. Thousands more died.

Japan's leaders knew they could not win the war. They surrendered on September 2, 1945, bringing an end to World War II.

The Tuskegee Airmen proved the experiment begun years before was a success. Skin color had nothing to do with bravery, intelligence, and teamwork. African Americans were as capable as any group of becoming superior soldiers and pilots.

The black pilots amassed a remarkable combat record. By the time pilot training ended in 1946 at Tuskegee, 993 pilots had graduated. About 450 of them had gone to Europe to fly in combat. Those pilots flew more than 1,500 missions.

Sixty-six of the black pilots died defending their country. Some others died in training accidents.

The black pilots downed 111 enemy planes in the air. They destroyed or damaged more than 270 aircraft on the ground and a number of boats, barges, and locomotives. They also sank one German destroyer.

"When the 99th first went [to Europe], the general impression was that it was an experiment," said pilot Lemuel Custis in a 1945 newspaper article. "Now I think the record shows it was a successful experiment."

Following the war, the black pilots went in many different directions. Some found jobs and others went to college.

Many were treated as heroes and honored in their hometowns.

"I noticed a change in the attitudes of whites after the medals were issued and we had the great war record," said Custis, one of the original Tuskegee Airmen.

Others were not treated well.

"When you arrived back in America, your uniform, rank, and medals meant little," said another Tuskegee Airman. "We were right back where we started."

Some of the black pilots and ground crew members remained in the military. The 477th, led by Colonel Davis, was assigned to Lockbourne Field near Columbus, Ohio. The all-black outfit was still facing troubles caused by segregation. Davis could not get enough qualified men.

In the summer of 1947, the 477th Composite Group became the 332nd Fighter Wing. The outfit was downsized because of continuing staffing problems. However, the military still resisted integration.

Harry S Truman

President Harry S Truman was aware of the racial problems in the service. He asked Congress to pass laws protecting the civil rights of all citizens. Frustrated by Congress's lack of action, Truman issued an executive order.

In July 1948, Truman signed Executive Order 9981. It called for the integration of the United States military.

Before long, members of the 332nd Fighter Wing were assigned to different wings. Later, all of the air force's black personnel were integrated into white units.

THE LATER YEARS

The Tuskegee Airmen left their mark on America after World War II. Many became high-ranking air force officers with long military careers. Others became outstanding businessmen and government workers. Some were elected to political offices.

Daniel "Chappie" James was a member of the 477th Bombardment Group during World War II. James stayed in the air force, becoming a combat pilot in both the Korean and Vietnam Wars.

In 1953, James became the first black to command an integrated combat outfit. In 1975, he became the nation's first African American four-star general.

Two other members of the 477th held highly visible positions. Coleman Young became mayor of Detroit, Michigan. William Coleman was named the U.S. Secretary of Transportation by President Gerald Ford.

It should be noted that James, Young, and Coleman were all arrested during the Freeman Field protest. Their strong belief in fairness and equality helped them become leaders in later life.

Roscoe Brown, a 332nd Fighter Group pilot, became president of a community college in New York City. Lemuel Custis was a state government official in Connecticut. Dr. Vance Marchbanks worked for the United States space program. And the list goes on.

Benjamin O. Davis, Jr., became the first black general in the air force in 1954. He later retired as a three-star general.

TUSKEGEE AIRMEN MEMORIALS

Several memorials are dedicated to the Tuskegee Airmen.

A statue of a Red Tail pilot is on display at the Air Force Academy in Colorado Springs, Colorado. A Tuskegee Airmen monument can be seen at the Air Force Museum, Wright-Patterson Air Force Base, Dayton, Ohio.

In Detroit, Michigan, visitors can see the National Museum of the Tuskegee Airmen.

The Tuskegee Airmen, Incorporated (TAI), is a national organization. Its members work to preserve the memory of the Tuskegee Airmen. TAI chapters are active in several cities.

After his distinguished military career, Davis became an assistant secretary at the U.S. Department of Transportation. He also held other important positions.

Davis's leadership made the Tuskegee experiment a success. Had he failed, military integration may have been delayed.

The Tuskegee Airmen helped the United States win the war in Europe. They also helped break down barriers for black citizens. They are truly American heroes.

GLOSSARY

discrimination   act of recognizing or giving different treatment based on something other than individual merit

integrate   to end segregation (see glossary entry) and bring together in society or an organization

morale   mental and emotional condition of an individual or group

prejudice   judgment or attitude against an individual, group, race, or their supposed characteristics

racism   belief that race determines human traits and that one race is superior to others

rookie   first-time participant

segregate   to separate or set apart from others or the general population

squadron   air force unit that is lower than a group

stamina   staying power or endurance

strafe   to destroy with machine-gun fire from low-flying aircraft

Index

Truman, Harry S, 58

Tuskegee, Alabama, 4, 7, 8, 9, 10,
    16, 17, 19, 20, 21, 22, 30, 31,
    41, 48, 56

Tuskegee Airmen, Incorporated
    (TAI), 60

Tuskegee Institute, 7, 8, 9–11, 16,
    17, 19, 20, 21, 27, 48

27th Fighter Group, 23–24

United States Air Force, 16

United States Army Air Corps
    (Force), 5, 6, 8, 11, 15, 16, 17,
    19, 28, 29, 30, 31, 33, 34, 45, 50

United States Military Academy
    (West Point), 10, 15, 18, 19

wars
        Civil, 5
        Korean, 59
        Revolutionary, 5
        Vietnam, 59
        War of 1812, 5
        World War I, 5, 13

Washington, Booker T., 9

Watson, Spann, 25

Weaver, Walter, 10

White, Sherman, 26

Young, Charles, 18

Young, Coleman, 59

Yugoslavia, 40, 46